Bitcoin

What you need to know about the cryptocurrency

By Mark Bresett

BONUS: DOWNLOAD MY
<u>FREE</u> BOOK

Thank you for purchasing my book.

I would like to offer you a FREE book *25 Ways to Build Wealth: Reach Your Ultimate Goal With These Smart, Simple Steps*.

To get this 100% free book, just visit my website:

www.Ways2BuildWealth.com/book

Table of Contents

Introduction

Congratulations on purchasing your personal copy of *Bitcoin: What you need to know about the cryptocurrency.* Thank you for doing so.

The following chapters will discuss some of the many aspects of Bitcoin and how they are used for different purposes.

You will discover how important it is to make sure that you jump on the Bitcoin train at just the right time so that you can make sure that you are going to be able to get the most out of the investment that you have made. Bitcoin prices have risen significantly and are still expected to come up in the coming years. Be prepared before there is a huge spike and you will not longer be able to afford them.

The final chapter will explore the things that you should look for when you are investing in Bitcoin and when you are working to build up your supply of Bitcoin.

There are plenty of books on this subject on the market, thanks again for choosing this one! Every effort was made to ensure it is full of as much useful information as possible.

Chapter 1
Defining Bitcoin

Bitcoin is, perhaps, the final frontier when it comes to currency in different areas around the world. It is a method of payment that does not discriminate between countries, rich, poor or anything else that could identify a person. Bitcoin was created to be able to trade money terms without ever having to use money and it is a perfect solution for the need to have something other than a typical bank for currency options. Those who use Bitcoin can understand how freeing it is to be able to rely on themselves instead of having to use the currency options that most banks have available for them.

Use

The availability of Bitcoin in major retail locations is something that is relatively new. Many people do not even know what Bitcoin is so it is somewhat hard for retailers to offer that as an option for the people who want to be able to use it.

Because it has become increasingly popular due to the fact that it is worth much more than what it once was, it has recently been featured at major retailers, like Overstock, a company that specializes in online sales and helps people who want to be able to purchase the majority of their necessities online.

The single biggest use of Bitcoin is from person to person. Second is from business to business and person to business or business to person comes in as the last spot for uses of Bitcoin in the sense of entity to entity.

Safety

Because of the way that Bitcoin is set up, it is much safer for people to use Bitcoin and other forms of cryptocurrency than it is for them to use traditional cash or even credit cards. Bitcoin is a type of currency that is exclusively online. Unless your wallet gets hacked by someone who wants to get your currency, there is virtually no way to have it stolen. Even if it does get hacked, it is encrypted so that it can be traced exactly back to the wallet that holds the Bitcoin that was stolen from you out of your own wallet.

Physical Attributes

There are, essentially, no physical attributes of Bitcoin. This is because the currency is exclusively online and it is more of an idea or a series of codes than anything else. Unlike cash or credit cards, you are not able to put the Bitcoin in your wallet and you cannot actually ever hold the currency in your hand.

This can be seen as both a good and bad thing – it is nearly impossible to lose it or steal it but you also are at the mercy of the computer system and the host that holds all of the codes for Bitcoin. What happens if it crashes?

Trades Between Countries

With more people getting involved in Bitcoin, it is easy for them to recognize that they are going to be able to use it for many different types of transactions. In the past, businesses or individuals who were in different countries had to wire money from person to person. It was complicated and the exchange rate got in the way of being able to get the exact amount to the other party. Now, with Bitcoin, everyone who uses it around the world uses the same form of currency. There is no need for exchange rates, bank transfers or even a wait time that is sometimes needed with money that is wired.

Anonymous Users

Perhaps one of the most popular aspects of Bitcoin, especially by those who used it in the early days, is the anonymity that comes with Bitcoin. While your name is technically attached to a wallet number, it is difficult to show your identity when you are using Bitcoin. If you want to be able to keep your identity secure and private, you will be able to do so with Bitcoin because of the different aspects that are included with your wallet. You're identified by a username or a wallet ID instead of being identified by your own name as you would be at a bank.

Chapter 2

Bitcoin Mastery

The idea behind Bitcoin is that it makes life easier for those who enjoy the Internet and technology. It is something that is helpful for many people but only if they know the right way to use it.

Anyone can go out and purchase Bitcoin but to really get the best use of Bitcoin and make money from it, you will need to make sure that you know the basics of it. Once you have discovered those (in Chapter 1), you will then be able to move onto Bitcoin mastery.

It does not take much to become a Bitcoin master and the following steps will teach you exactly what you need to make sure that you are going to be able to become the best that you can be when you are dealing with Bitcoin.

Purchase of Bitcoin

The single most popular option for purchasing Bitcoin is to buy it from a site or app like Coin Base. This is a company that deals only in Bitcoin and they rule the market so that people can make sure that they are getting the best experience possible with Bitcoin. It is something that they have worked hard to build up and something that most people who use Bitcoin trust to be able to buy their Bitcoin from.

When you buy your Bitcoin from Coin Base, you will have many different options to choose from. You can simply use your credit or debit card to buy the Bitcoin or you can choose to use a bank account. With a bank account, as long as Coin Base can verify it, you will be able to buy a much larger amount of Bitcoin at one time because of the parameters that are set up with Bank accounts.

It is a good idea to try and make sure that you know where you are going to buy from. While Coin Base is the most popular option for people to buy Bitcoin from, you can also choose other sites to purchase from. Before the Silk Road was shut down by the FBI, there were hundreds of places to buy Bitcoin – now, there is only a handful.

Coin Base seems to be the best option for those who are just getting started with Bitcoin because you can buy, trade and even sell your Bitcoin right from the app.

Getting Rid of Bitcoin

At some point, you will probably want to offload some of the Bitcoin that you have. Most people do this from an investment perspective and you should only do it when you know that you are going to be able to profit from it. This is an important factor of Bitcoin and something that you will need to keep in mind before you sell it off.

The one way that you can get rid of your Bitcoin is to use it for purchases but that will cause you to not get the most value out of your Bitcoin.

Selling it is the best way to get a return on your Bitcoin investment and it is something that you need to do if you want to make money. You can sell right through Coin Base so that you can get the amount returned on the investment that you have made. Another way that you can make money from Bitcoin is simply selling to another individual. You may not get as much as what you would like for it but you will not have to worry about the fees that come with selling on Coin Base.

Where You Can Use Bitcoin

There are a few places online that you can use Bitcoin. These places are increasing and even some big name brand companies have started to use Bitcoin as a form of currency. Places like Overstock.com and even Facebook allow you to pay for goods and services on them. This is something that is much different from what was allowed in previous years.

If you are hoping to use your Bitcoin for *everything* that you purchase online, you can use one of the many Bitcoin marketplaces. These are set up in a similar fashion to an online store but you can use your Bitcoin to buy everything from a new house to a hover board to even services that you can use in real life. The biggest differences in these Bitcoin marketplaces is that the only form of currency accepted at each of them is Bitcoin. You can't just use your credit card to pay and you must have a Bitcoin wallet number to even be able to enter the marketplace where you purchase these items.

Investment of Bitcoin

Most people who choose to use Bitcoin are actually doing so as an investment. They don't do it so that they can buy things online and they certainly don't do it to join the marketplaces but they, instead, do it so that they can make the most out of the money that they have invested in it. Similar to other types of trades, people who invest in Bitcoin are actually able to sell it off for a profit later on. The people who initially invested in Bitcoin are actually making huge profits because of the change in the price of Bitcoin.

Changes in Price

As the market has changed and Bitcoin has become increasingly popular, the price has skyrocketed. What was originally not worth much is now worth a large amount. In fact, Bitcoin is one of the fastest (and largest per margin) growing investments that have made their way onto the market in the past 20 years. It is something that has been able to grow from a very small amount of money to a much larger amount and people are learning that they stand to make a lot of money from the investments.

The change in price all depends on the popularity of the investment. The more popular something is, the more it increases in price. Bitcoin is no different. As the demand for it rises, the price increases. There is no shortage of supply of Bitcoin but it is something that is going to continue to rise because of the huge demand that is out there for it. Just 10 years ago, nobody had ever heard of Bitcoin. Now, about 50% of people have heard about it and even more want in on the action. With a market that is nearly impossible to saturate, Bitcoin is expected to increase in price for years to come.

Organically Finding Bitcoin

You don't have to just rely on buying Bitcoin. Some of the biggest Bitcoin owners in the world have actually found their own Bitcoin without paying any money for it. This is through the process of mining. While you will learn a lot more about mining in the next chapter, it is important for you to know that buying it isn't the only way to get it and those who choose to mine Bitcoin are actually able to make decent profits off of the Bitcoin that they have found all on their own.

Your Wallet

The wallet that you have for your Bitcoin is something that is very important. This is where you hold the Bitcoin but it is also where all of your transactions will happen. In the world of Bitcoin, you are nothing more than a wallet. This is because you need your wallet ID to make trades, buy Bitcoin and even sell it off for a profit. If you want to purchase anything, at all, with Bitcoin, you need to have a wallet along with a wallet ID that will tie you to the Bitcoin that you have built up in that same wallet.

Chapter 3
Finding Your Own Bitcoin

This chapter will likely be the most complicated one when it comes to Bitcoin. This is because there is no specific explanation of how Bitcoin mining works and what it can do for people who choose to use it. There are many different ways to mine for Bitcoin and some people have found that other methods work better than what works for other people. While mining Bitcoin can be very profitable, it is something that you should only attempt if you have the technological and mathematical know-how along with the ability to spend a lot of time looking for it.

With Bitcoin mining, it is possible to make a lot of money but you must invest a lot of time. For example, some people will spend up to an entire week just to be able to find a single Bitcoin.

Community Aspect

There is a strong community that surrounds Bitcoin. This is due to the fact that only a small percentage of the world's population knows what Bitcoin is, how to use it or even owns some of the Bitcoin. Because of the small community, they all work together to get things done.

For Bitcoin to be able to work, there need to be certain mathematical problems that are solved. These are all created through the use of algorithms and they make the money encrypted. If miners are able to do this, they can find the code for the Bitcoin.

The community made it so that anyone would be able to mine for it. This allows the codes to get solved but it also gives people the motivation that they need to be able to find their own Bitcoin. Even those who are broke can start investing in Bitcoin but they have to have the know-how.

The Basics

When someone wants to be able to mine Bitcoin, they simply have to go into the database and do many searches for the problems that need to be solved. These are complicated and they may end up solving and sifting through hundreds of them before they find one that will turn into a Bitcoin code. It is something that, if done manually, would take thousands upon thousands of hours to even find one. When Bitcoin first started, it was much simpler.

After people learned about mining, they decided to start creating machines that would give them the chance to be able to mine for the Bitcoin that they wanted. This was all computer work and often involved building their own systems so that they could create the perfect mining machines. It is something that people still do and the majority of miners have systems that they have created for the sole purpose of finding Bitcoin. They have entire computers and network systems that are dedicated to being able to mine Bitcoin.

The machines are often built from scratch and involve the use of the Raspberry Pi systems which allow people to build their own programs.

As a Miner

The majority of miners who try to find Bitcoin started out as a hobby. After they found their first Bitcoin, they were able to then build from there with the money that they made. It was something that gave them the motivation that they needed to be able to find Bitcoin. Some people have such in depth systems that are so good at finding Bitcoin that they are Bitcoin miners on a full-time basis and that is how they make their money. They then are able to invest their earnings because Bitcoin is something that is always going up in value.

Many of the miners who are now finding large numbers of Bitcoin on a regular basis are ones who originally started out with mining. Around 50% of the people who are now mining for Bitcoin were among the first people who were mining Bitcoin. They have learned how to find the best math problems, create the algorithms and get the most amount of money from the Bitcoin that they have found.

Help from Bitcoin

While there is no way for Bitcoin to actually help the miners out with the searches that they are doing, it is something that people can find benefits from. The more Bitcoin that they have, the more that they can benefit from the different computer systems that they are able to afford to build when they are doing different things.

Having a lot of money in Bitcoin does not necessarily make it easier for people to find more Bitcoin but it does give them the chance to be able to make more complicated and in depth machines. When they are able to have the most sophisticated machine, they will also be able to get the most Bitcoin from using the machine to mine.

The creators of Bitcoin have very little to do with the cryptocurrency now. Even if they were heavily involved, they would not know all of the answers to the mathematical problems. That is because they designed Bitcoin in a way that allows them to give everyone equal chances to be able to find the money. As long as someone has the skill to build the machine and the know how to solve the problems that are included with most Bitcoin mining opportunities, they can invest in Bitcoin and make money from that investment.

Bitcoin is truly an equal opportunity.

You Need Hardware

There is almost no way to mine for Bitcoin without hardware with all of the people who are currently mining for it. In the past, people were able to mine it manually, solve the problems and even find it in different areas. That is not the case anymore and it is something that can be really detrimental for those who do not have the hardware to be able to find it. There is no way to make a sustainable income through the use of Bitcoin mining.

The good news, though, is that if you have one Bitcoin or even if you have somehow managed to spend an outrageous amount of time looking for a single Bitcoin, you do have the money to create your own machine. In general, getting a Raspberry Pi system and setting it up to be able to use should only cost you a couple hundred dollars – far less than the 2017 price of Bitcoin.

Finding one Bitcoin or purchasing one can then lead to you having the financial ability to be able to set up your own mining machine and finding a lot of Bitcoin that you can then make money from.

Starting Out

Most people who start out will have computer-based knowledge. They will know how to set up hardware and they will have an idea of what it takes to be able to get the different aspects of mining done for Bitcoin.

If you are going to mine the Bitcoin, it is worth looking at different options. There are many sites where you can practice the mining process and these sites will give you a good idea of what you will be able to do with the Bitcoin that you have or that you are going to be looking for.

Always make sure that you are really ready to start mining Bitcoin. It is not only an investment that you will need to make with the money that you have but it is also a huge time investment. You should be prepared to spend a lot of time looking for Bitcoin and trying to build the machines that will help you to find Bitcoin. No matter where you are or what you do with Bitcoin, you cannot just jump right into mining.

Learn as much as you can about Bitcoin mining and then try your hand at it to avoid wasted time and money.

Chapter 4
Bitcoin Trading Process

All Bitcoin really involves in trading. Since it is not an actual officially accepted currency, people can just trade for Bitcoin and trade their Bitcoin for different things. There are many different ways that you can trade your Bitcoin and different things that you can do. Bitcoin is good for trading everything from cash to homes and even small goods like groceries. If you are going to use Bitcoin for trading purposes, you need to be sure that you are doing it the right way and that you are not losing out on money as a result of the trades that you are making with the Bitcoin that you have in your own possession.

For Services

The majority of services that you can trade for Bitcoin are online-based services. Some people who use Bitcoin will choose to trade it for:

- Website creation

- Content marketing

- Site enhancement

- Computer optimization

Because Bitcoin is a computer-based currency and something that people can trade online, it is something that has a lot of use in the online world. In the past, people who were doing each of these things and trading them for other things would actually have to pay for them using a credit card (which can be risky) or using a payment service, like Paypal (which can be extremely complicated).

The introduction of Bitcoin makes it much easier for people to try and pay for the services that they have online. It is something that everyone is able to benefit from. Even if you don't have a website, you don't have any use for content marketing or you don't want to create a website at any point, you can use Bitcoin to trade for a service that will help make your computer run better than what it ever had before.

By using each of these services, you will enable yourself to have a better computer or technology experience. If you want to be able to make the experience even better, you can choose to trade it for Bitcoin so that you have to take one less step to be able to pay for those services. Bitcoin makes it easy to pay and even communicate with the people who are going to provide those services to you.

For Goods

There are many goods that you can purchase online. The majority of these goods are found at online retailers and many of the biggest retailers in the online world have now started to accept Bitcoin as a form of payment. You can use your Bitcoin wallet at the most popular retailers and that will enable you to have an easier and more secure online shopping experience. To be able to use your Bitcoin at an online retailer:

1. Find what you are looking for and add everything that you want to purchase into your shopping cart or shopping bag on the retailer's site

2. Go to the cart or bag and review the things that you are buying

3. Use the checkout button that is provided

4. Find the place where you can pay with Bitcoin

5. Enter your personal information so that your items can be shipped to you

6. Find the place and enter your Bitcoin wallet ID so that you can pay for the items

7. Confirm the purchase

Your Bitcoin wallet will automatically be updated with the information on the purchase and it will be deducted the amount that you just purchased your items for. You do not have to wait for a statement or anything to clear because it does it all instantly.

Traditional Trades

Bitcoin is a great thing to have when you are doing trade investments. These are the type of investments that include things like stocks, bonds, and even mutual funds. You can do the same thing with your Bitcoin and simply purchase them for investment purposes.

If you were going to invest in something else or even if you were going to hang onto the money in the form of traditional cash in a savings account, it would take years to build up a return on the total amount that you put into the account. The percentages of even high-interest savings accounts are much lower than the return that you will get on the Bitcoin that you invested in.

Another great aspect of trading in an investment sense with Bitcoin is that you do not have to put it in a specific account to build up the value of it. All you need to do is allow it to sit in your wallet that the rest of your Bitcoin is in. This will allow it to build up in value as the Bitcoin continues to grow, as a whole, in value. Within a year, there is a chance that you could make back up to 25% (or more) of your investment.

When You Purchase

When you buy your Bitcoin, you need to make sure that you buy it at a good time. On the weekends and in the early morning before the market opens for the day is the best time to buy your Bitcoin. This is something that you will need to do to make sure that you are getting the best price. Watch the prices of Bitcoin for a few days and see when it is the lowest.

If you buy your Bitcoin at the lowest point within five days, you will be able to automatically make a return on that investment so that you can make sure that you are actually making money from the Bitcoin. It is a good idea to only buy it when it is as low as possible. If you think of the people who initially bought Bitcoin, they likely only spent a few dollars for Bitcoin that is now worth millions of dollars today.

Buying at the right time will have a huge impact on your ability to profit with Bitcoin.

When you Sell It

Opposite of when you are buying Bitcoin, you need to watch out for the highest price when you are selling it. You also need to keep in mind the selling fee if you are trying to sell it on a site like Coin Base because you could end up *losing* money on the sale if you don't do it at the right time. By selling it when it is at its highest, you will be able to make the profits that you need to be able to buy more Bitcoin and turn around to do the same thing.

If you sell your Bitcoin when it is at the highest price possible, the chance that it is going to drop again is good and it is something that you need to remember when you are selling. After you have sold it, monitor the price for a few days. Use the profits that you made from the sale to buy more of the lower-priced Bitcoin. This is the easiest way to make a lot of money from Bitcoin and it is also the fastest. There is no long waiting period in between when you buy and sell the Bitcoin so you can make profits fast.

Swapping Bitcoin

While you already know that you can trade Bitcoin for goods and services, you can also trade Bitcoin in a different way on the Internet. If you are using Bitcoin, you can trade it for other Bitcoin, for different types of cryptocurrency or even for different things that you have. For example, if you have something that is very unique or rare, you can actually use it to barter for Bitcoin.

Since Bitcoin is not an official currency and it is not regulated, you can use it for almost anything. That means that you can ask someone for three Bitcoin for a book that you have and they want. There is no guidelines for trading or for selling things with Bitcoin so keep that in mind when *you* are the one who is trying to get Bitcoin. It can be complicated to figure out what you should pay or what you should accept as payment.

When you are using Bitcoin, always be careful because it is not regulated. While you can get a lot of "money" for things that aren't quite worth that large of an amount, you also have the chance of getting ripped off with Bitcoin. Always know the value of things that you are buying and selling as well as the value of Bitcoin at that point in time.

Chapter 5
Changing Values of Bitcoin

When Bitcoin was first brought on as a type of cryptocurrency (one of the first, actually), it was not worth much. Many people did not think that it was going to last and some even thought that they would lose money by investing in it. Others, though, believed in the idea of it and they invested in it. Those people were smart because the Bitcoin that they invested so little in just eight years ago is now worth a lot of money. For just a few dollars, they are now millionaires.

Year 2009

Average Bitcoin Price: .0001 American Dollars

If you owned 10 Bitcoin, you would have: .001 worth of Bitcoin, less than one cent

Years on the market: 0

The people who first invested in Bitcoin did not pay much for the amount that they had. In fact, people who invested 10 dollars actually got 100,000 Bitcoin. They did not know at the time but they would eventually be able to see a huge return on that money.

While 10 dollars would have gotten you a lot of Bitcoin during that time, people who really believed in the idea behind Bitcoin actually invested a lot more than just 10 dollars. Some invested hundreds, even thousands of dollars into Bitcoin. They didn't know at the time but they were actually helping to increase the value of Bitcoin and inflate the price of it by doing this.

Year 2010

Average Bitcoin Price: .07 American Dollars

If you owned 10 Bitcoin, you would have: .7 worth of Bitcoin, just under one dollar

Years on the market: 1

This was the first of many huge increases in Bitcoin in the past eight years. It started out at far less than one cent and the price was driven upward by investors and those who wanted to be able to get in on the Bitcoin game. This is the point that many people saw that Bitcoin may not be such a joke after all. While the seven cent price point was not huge and was actually far less than some of the other investment options that were on the market, it was a huge increase.

Good investors were able to realize this and started to invest even more money into Bitcoin. The average purchase of Bitcoin often involved thousands of dollars. The people who were doing this were not big-name investors but were, instead, technology aficionados who wanted to be able to get in on the action.

Still, at this point in time, if you had 10 dollars to spare, you could get yourself 142 Bitcoin. Those who did this during that time were wise.

Year 2011

Average Bitcoin Price: 15 American Dollars

If you owned 10 Bitcoin, you would have: 150 dollars' worth of Bitcoin

Years on the market: 2

This was the second time during the lifespan of Bitcoin that it took another huge jump in price. It was something that was propelled by the investors who were spending thousands of dollars to be able to get into the Bitcoin game and it was something that also allowed them the chance to make sure that they were going to be able to have a lot of money later on.

By this point, most investors realized that Bitcoin was going to stay on the market. They knew that it was something that had the potential to change the way that the stock market worked in a huge way and that it was going to be able to be one of the fastest growing investment opportunities in the world.

Year 2012

Average Bitcoin Price: 7 American Dollars

If you owned 10 Bitcoin, you would have: 70 dollars' worth of Bitcoin

Years on the market: 3

For the very first time in its short history, Bitcoin dropped in price. Compared to the huge increases that it had in the past, this was a relatively large dip but it was something that was to be expected considering that Bitcoin had only been on the market for a short period of time. In fact, the 7 dollar price point was something that many people thought the Bitcoin would peak at.

People began to back out. They sold off their Bitcoin in fear that it would drop again in the coming months.

The smart investors, though, knew that there was always a drop in price before there was another huge increase. They held onto the Bitcoin. They waited it out and the patience that they had for the market that they had chosen to join paid off for them.

Year 2013

Average Bitcoin Price: 100 American Dollars

If you owned 10 Bitcoin, you would have: 1,000 dollars' worth of Bitcoin

Years on the market: 4

Those who held onto their Bitcoin during the drop in price were rejoicing because they knew that they had made the right decision by keeping the Bitcoin that they had. It was important that they kept it because it allowed them to have a much larger amount of Bitcoin.

While these people felt that they were able to be blessed because they had a lot of Bitcoin, those who had purchased it back in 2009 were even better off. If you had purchased 10 dollars worth of Bitcoin in 2009, you would have been a millionaire in 2013. There were actually more than a few people who reached that point. Many of them cashed out at that point – satisfied with the fact that they had made a million and wanting to pull out before they lost money. Still, others stayed. Many figured that it couldn't get much worse than that initial 10 dollar investment.

Year 2014

Average Bitcoin Price: 600 American Dollars

If you owned 10 Bitcoin, you would have: 6,000 dollars' worth of Bitcoin

Years on the market: 5

This was another increase but not a huge one that had been seen in the early days. While it was smaller than those times, it was a big increase and it propelled those had bought during the 2009 Bitcoin selling season to be multimillionaires.

Again, more people cashed in on the Bitcoin that they had. They wanted to get out before it was too late. This was especially true of those who had multi-millions of dollars at stake.

Year 2015

Average Bitcoin Price: 220 American Dollars

If you owned 10 Bitcoin, you would have: 2,200 dollars' worth of Bitcoin

Years on the market: 6

During this time, the illegal market that was running on the Internet, the Silk Road, was seized and closed. It was a time that hurt a lot of people who dealt exclusively in Bitcoin and it caused the price to drop.

The seasoned investors knew that this was bound to happen so they did not let it get in the way of their investments. They wanted to continue cashing in on Bitcoin so they did just that. They left their Bitcoin in their wallets and did not sell just because of the drop. They hoped that it would rise again.

2016

Average Bitcoin Price: 1,146 American Dollars

If you owned 10 Bitcoin, you would have: 11,460 dollars' worth of Bitcoin

Years on the market: 7

For the first time in a long time, Bitcoin more than tripled in value. Those who had bought 10 dollars worth of Bitcoin in 2009, now had a wallet that was worth over one hundred thousand dollars. The thing, though, was that people who had bought all of those shares up in 2009 actually spent thousands of dollars on Bitcoin. The year 2016 was celebratory for them in that they passed the billion dollar mark. While they have it all divided up into different wallets, they are still billionaires.

2017

Average Bitcoin Price: 992 American dollars (as of January)

If you owned 10 Bitcoin, you would have: 9,920 dollars' worth of Bitcoin

Years on the market: 8

While there was a slight drop at the beginning of the year, it is expected that Bitcoin is going to pass the price of gold in the coming months. It is expected to hover around the $1,000 mark for a few months and then shoot up to nearly $2,000.

There is no way to determine the exact amount, but some people expect Bitcoin to reach a value of over $10,000 by the time that we reach 2020.

If you haven't already, *now* is the time to buy Bitcoin so that you can cash in later.

Chapter 6
Buying with Bitcoin

Buying items or services with Bitcoin may not be the best way to use the Bitcoin that you have but it is something that can help you gain access to things that people can only purchase with Bitcoin. If you have Bitcoin in your possession, it may not be a bad idea to set some aside so that you can purchase different items with them. Investing is one of the easiest ways to make money but you should learn how to buy things that are fun with Bitcoin, too.

Everyday Purchases

You and make everyday purchases with the Bitcoin that you have in your possession. This can be anything from buying a pack of phone chargers to being able to purchase your toilet paper from an online retailer. Those who use Bitcoin for everyday purchases often have a lot of Bitcoin. It just makes more sense for them to use the Bitcoin to buy the things that they need instead of having to cash it in or sell it off and then using the cash to be able to buy these items.

On top of the convenience that comes with *not* having to sell the Bitcoin, those who purchase using Bitcoin also save money when it comes to the seller fees that they would normally incur.

Retailers Who Take It

Major online retailers are now accepting Bitcoin as a form of payment for their customers. Aside from Overstock.com that we already discussed, there are also a few others that accept your Bitcoin as a form of payment:

* Dish TV – a subscription television service. You can pay your bill, buy pay per view shows and even add features to your television service with Bitcoin. This is the only television service that offers it.

* Expedia – one of the premier travel sites and the only one that people who pay in Bitcoin are able to use. You can book a flight, a hotel, a car and even tours on the site. When you have chosen the travel options that you want, you can pay using Bitcoin.

* eGifter – the premier option for people who *only* have Bitcoin to spend. On this site, you can buy gift cards worth more than the amount that you are paying (or, rarely, the same). You can then pay with Bitcoin so that you can use your gift cards at places that *don't* take Bitcoin. This is one way that many Bitcoin big shots choose to spend their Bitcoin so that they can avoid the seller fees that come with Bitcoin wallet administrators.

Buying Offline

There are not many retailers who offer Bitcoin as an option online and there are even fewer who offer the option to purchase with Bitcoin in an offline format.

As of 2017, there are no major retailers who have the capability of accepting Bitcoin offline. They would require special machines that would simply be too costly for them to install in all locations.

There are some offline retailers, though, that allow customers to pay in Bitcoin. The majority of these are niche shops.

One option that retailers do have is if they use the Shopify platform, they can offer Bitcoin payment options to their customers through that service. There, the customers can use the checkout process (online or off) and decide whether they want to pay with their Bitcoin wallet.

Bitcoin-Only

There are some places that do not offer any other option than paying in Bitcoin. These are generally market-style websites and places that will identify themselves as Bitcoin-only locations. You can make sure that you are in one of these places because of the many sellers who use these platforms. If you are hoping to gain some form of Bitcoin, you can also use one of these marketplaces to sell the things that you have to offer — many Bitcoin owners got started this way.

Be aware that to be able to use these sites and the marketplaces that accompany them, you will need to have a wallet identification number that you can use to make sure that you have Bitcoin before you can even get into the site.

Huge Purchases

There are people who have purchased homes using only Bitcoin. These, of course, are people who have the ability to purchase a home without a mortgage but they are able to do so with the Bitcoin similar to how other people would pay cash to be able to buy a house. One of the most expensive houses that was ever purchased with Bitcoin went for over one million dollars.

The chances are pretty high that the purchaser of the home (or the seller) was one of the original Bitcoin owners.

The Silk Road

Before its closure and subsequent investigations in 2015, the Silk Road was the number one place to buy and sell using Bitcoin. Thousands of people used the site to trade on a regular basis and they did many different things with the Bitcoin that they had.

People who used the Silk Road could purchase anything from illegal marijuana to black market copies of movies that were not even released on DVD yet. Some of the purchases were simple and only "illegal" because they needed to be moderated by the government. Others, like human trafficking victims, were illegal *and* immoral.

Unusual Purchases

One of the most unusual purchases, or extravagant, with Bitcoin, was the purchase of a helicopter. While the specific details of the purchase and the person who made, the purchase were not revealed, the people who did it are alleged friends and have been in the Bitcoin market for as long as it has existed. There's a strong possibility that it was also one of the parties that was involved in the house purchase...or at least someone who knows one of those people because the Bitcoin world is a tight community.

Technology Purchases

While this fact may be unsurprising, especially after learning all about the Bitcoin and technology connection, the majority of purchases that are made with Bitcoin are for technology-related purposes. These purchases can be anything from the latest gadgets to new and improved ways of doing different things within the technology community. It is important to note that not *all* Bitcoin purchases or trades have to be related to the Internet and technology but that a large portion of them are since Bitcoin is an online-only concept of money and trading.

Buying More Bitcoin

Some people have chosen to buy more Bitcoin just so they can make purchases.

While it is a great idea to buy more Bitcoin, especially if you are going to invest it, it may not be the best idea to buy it for the sole purpose of purchasing things on the Internet or even off of the Internet. Since Bitcoin is constantly fluctuating, it is hard to set an accurate price on items that are being sold for Bitcoin. You may end up losing money by using your Bitcoin for purchases.

The only way to make sure that you are not getting ripped off with Bitcoin and buying goods and services is to have a lot of Bitcoin. When you reach a certain amount, it is more profitable for you to simply buy items with Bitcoin instead of selling it with the seller's fee that is involved.

Dividing the Bitcoin

Since quite a few things cost far less than $1,000, there is a system for dividing Bitcoin. People who invest can even get involved in this and buy just a *portion* of a Bitcoin at a time. This makes it easier to invest and to actually pay for things with Bitcoin so that people do not have to lose the total amount that they purchased when they originally had the Bitcoin.

Chapter 7
Bitcoin and the Government

By now, you're probably wondering who has the most amount of Bitcoin in the world. There are many people who own Bitcoin and there are a lot of people who have hundreds of thousands and millions of dollars worth of Bitcoin. These are mostly people who started in the game early and who grew their Bitcoin profits from the simple .0001 cents that each Bitcoin was originally worth.

What you may be surprised to find out is that not a single one of those people are actually the biggest Bitcoin holder in the world. In fact, the chances are that you would never even *guess* who is the biggest owner of Bitcoin in the world. Don't worry, though, you'll know by the end of the chapter after we finish discussing how Bitcoin and the United States government fit together.

Government Regulation

There is currently no regulation of Bitcoin from the United States government or any government. This is because Bitcoin is a fairly new concept and it is designed to work more like something that people own instead of something that people use as a way to pay for things.

There is always a chance that the government will begin to regulate Bitcoin but it generally takes over a decade to regulate different forms of currency. In the past, it took a long time to make the switch and then the government was not able to regulate two different types of currency so they had to choose one. The chances of Bitcoin being chosen are very slim.

When the government makes the decision to regulate Bitcoin, they will need to figure out how they are going to make it less anonymous and they will have to make sure that they are prepared for the pushback that will come from the people who currently own Bitcoin.

It is a product that can be traded, not something that can be spent.

Not Currency

The United States government currently works hard to make sure that it is clear that Bitcoin is not actual currency. It is simply something that people can use to trade for different things. They may pay money to be able to have it but, to the government, this is no different than paying money to buy stocks in a company or to buy into something that is just an idea.

There are some small regulations that come along with this type of trade and with people being able to buy into Bitcoin but it is nothing compared to the type of regulations that come along with currency. The government has very little control over what people are able to do with Bitcoin, how much they are able to be worth and how much different Bitcoin sellers are able to charge for the Bitcoin that people are buying from them.

In fact, it is such an unregulated type of trading that some conservatives think of Bitcoin as the black market.

Since it's not actually illegal and is on the up and up with the stock market, there is no way that Bitcoin is black market.

Owners of Bitcoin

In the past, people who owned a lot of Bitcoin were monitored by the government very closely. This was something that came along with those same people being watched for silk-road related purposes. The majority of people who had a lot of Bitcoin in one wallet were the ones who were not doing things that were legal and who were participating on the Silk Road.

Many people who own Bitcoin know better, though. They know that they should keep their Bitcoin in different wallets. Because of this, it appears that many more people own Bitcoin than what was originally thought. This is especially true of the people who have had Bitcoin since it first started. Each one has multiple wallets that they work from so it is nearly impossible to judge how much Bitcoin each of the people has.

This also makes it more difficult to track them, contributing even further to the idea that Bitcoin is focused on the anonymity of the people who use it and that it is something that anyone with an email address and a bank account is able to access without having to give up the specific details of their identity.

Problems from Government

The biggest problem that comes for Bitcoin is from the government aspect of it. The problem is because the government does not regulate it and they currently have no way to do so. Because of this, they look down on the use of Bitcoin. The government has no say-so in how Bitcoin is handled, what it can be used for and the way that it is able to be sold. Because of this, the government has worked hard to shut down the operations of Bitcoin.

In 2015, when the Silk Road was seized, they actually thought that they had shut down Bitcoin. They found a lot of Bitcoin during that time and they believed that it was all of the Bitcoin in the world. What they didn't know, though, was that Bitcoin was used in other areas aside from the Silk Road. Bitcoin still existed even after the Silk Road shut down.

Shut Down of the Silk Road

As 2015 came to a close and the trials began for the Silk Road, the FBI found that they had a problem on their hand: Bitcoin. It wasn't necessarily illegal to have like some of the other digital property that the people who were on the Silk Road owned but it was somewhat of a conundrum for the people who seized all of the things that came off of the Silk Road.

The FBI had no idea what to do with it.

As they continued to work on the Silk Road and seize different things from it, they took more and more from the biggest players on the Silk Road. They worked to make sure that they had everything that the people who had worked on the Silk Road had and they did everything that they could to make sure that there was nothing left. This included the seizure of the Bitcoin that people had paid in on the Silk Road.

The FBI is the biggest owner of Bitcoin thanks to the seizure of the Silk Road. Since Bitcoin *seemed* like property and really had no official classification, the FBI seized them as if they were property. The FBI currently holds 144,000 Bitcoin. That number is worth over 100 thousand American Dollars.

* Note: while the FBI is the official owner of the largest collection of Bitcoin, the chances that someone else has an even larger collection are high. Since so many people who use Bitcoin choose to keep it in separate wallets, it is impossible to tell how many wallets are assigned to each person. One person could have 30 wallets that each have 20 thousand Bitcoin in them. Because of this, there is reason to believe that the creator of Bitcoin, whose official identity has never been revealed, has the largest collection and has over 50 wallets that the Bitcoin are all stored in.

Chapter 8

Bitcoin for Investment

Now that you know how much Bitcoin can increase in just less than a decade, it is clear to see how great of an investment it can be. For this reason, many people choose to use it as an investment instead of simply purchasing it for their own use. The investment aspect of Bitcoin is one of the most profitable options for the people who use Bitcoin. It is a great way for you to make money and you may even be able to make passive income from it if you know the right way to be able to use it to your advantage.

Getting Your Own

The cheapest but most time intensive method of getting Bitcoin is through mining. You will need to learn the technology-related skills that go along with mining and the math skills that come with having the ability to make sure that you are solving each of the problems that come up with the algorithms included in mining. It is a good idea to be sure that you are ready to invest in the time that it takes to be able to mine.

Once you are sure that you are going to be able to mine and you know all of the different aspects of it, you can prepare to mine the Bitcoin that you want to be able to invest in.

By investing your time in mining, you will be able to make a 100% profit on the monetary value of the Bitcoin that you find while you are mining it.

Keeping the Coin

Once you have Bitcoin, you should hold onto it so that it can increase in value. The people who did this in 2009 are now millionaires with many of them reaching the billion dollar mark. It will take some patience to be able to hold onto your Bitcoin for a few years but it will certainly be worth it when you can sell it for nearly ten times the amount that you bought it for. During this time, you will not be able to collect on the return of the Bitcoin but you will be able to make sure that you get the right amount in the end.

Selling It Off

If you currently have Bitcoin, you can sell it to make money. Even if you don't have a full Bitcoin value and only have a portion of it, you will be able to make a profit on it. It won't be as much as it would be if you were selling off a large amount of Bitcoin but it will be able to help you if you need to collect on the returns that you have with the Bitcoin.

In general, it is a good idea to wait as long as possible before you sell off the Bitcoin. Because of the different problems that come along with the sale of Bitcoin, you should always make sure that you are going to make the most amount of profit.

This is a great idea for people who have a lot of Bitcoin. For example, someone who has 10 Bitcoin right now and needs some money out of the returns from the Bitcoin can simply sell one of them. They will be able to collect on the profit of that single one but will also be able to keep the other nine so that they can continue to grow in value.

Merchant Acceptance

Have you ever wondered what makes those who offer Bitcoin as a form of payment different from those who do not? The difference lies in the profits that those who do are able to make from the Bitcoin. When merchants offer the option for customers to pay with Bitcoin, they will then be able to keep that Bitcoin to themselves. They can invest the Bitcoin by simply letting it sit and grow or they can sell it off for a profit, often within a short period of time.

If you have something that you can sell – whether it is a good or a service – you can offer the option for people to pay in Bitcoin. When someone pays with Bitcoin simply keep it and then invest it back into the business. You can make a lot more money from Bitcoin than you can from having to pay credit card processing fees.

Offering Bitcoin as a payment option for your customers is a win-win situation and will allow you to keep more of your profits *and* build up even more profits from the Bitcoin that will eventually grow in value.

Trading Through the Day

Day trading is not a new concept. In fact, it is something that people are able to do in nearly all aspects of trading and with all of the different investments that they make. Day trading is the idea that you buy and sell off the stocks or other investment opportunities that you have within one day's time. From the time that the market opens until it closes, you would constantly be selling and buying up the different things that you have.

You can also do this with Bitcoin. All you need to do is start the day out by buying the Bitcoin that you want. Throughout the day, the price will fluctuate. It will increase as the day goes on and you will be able to buy and sell the Bitcoin so that you can make a profit on it. By the end of the day, you should have been able to build up a decent amount of money in profits. The profits are relatively small compared to what you would see by holding onto it but it goes much quicker. The price can fluctuate as much as 100 dollars throughout the day.

This is a fast paced type of investing and something that you should be able to dedicate a lot of time to throughout the day.

Increasing Your Money

The money that you make from Bitcoin can always be increased. It is something that you will simply have to do so that you will be able to increase the profits that you have.

If you find that you have made profit on Bitcoin, always try to put that money back into your investments. Whether you put it back into Bitcoin or you choose a different investment option, you will be able to make the most amount of money from investing it.

Wise investors know that they can continue to invest in all of the profits that they have. They know that constantly investing their profits is the best way to make money and it will allow them the chance to build up, even more, money than what they had before.

The only way that you can make passive income with Bitcoin is if you continue to purchase the Bitcoin that you need. Each time that you reinvest the money that you have made from Bitcoin, you will be one step closer to being completely independent with the Bitcoin that you have made. It will make things much easier for you to make real money and have a chance at the best monetary values possible.

Chapter 9

Tips and Fun Facts About Bitcoin

Bitcoin is clearly a great way to make money and is something that is a technological revolution. It was created for simple purposes but it has grown into so much more. Because of the way that people are able to use Bitcoin, there are a few things that you should look for when you are shopping for Bitcoin and when you are using Bitcoin in different instances.

The Lowest Price

Always look for the lowest price possible when it comes to Bitcoin and buying it. Keep track of the prices and get predictions for what the price is going to be like. While there is no way to be certain how far the price is going to go up (or down), you can do certain things to make sure that you are watching the patterns. This will give you a great chance at being able to get the lowest price and to always make sure that it is going to be the best investment for you.

If you see that Bitcoin is at the lowest price throughout the day, you should take the time and buy it at that point. The chances are that it will go back up and you will not be able to get that same price again so that you will need to make sure that you are going to get more out of the Bitcoin and that you will not have to make as big of an investment in the Bitcoin that you have.

Getting Bitcoin for the lowest price possible is a key part of making sure that you can truly get a good return on your investment.

The Highest Price

The highest price will always be the best price for you to make sure that you are getting a good return on your investment.

If you find that you are not going to be able to sell it for what you paid for, wait until you are able to sell it for that price or more. The people who waited out the time periods where Bitcoin was taking huge drops in price were then able to make up for it when it went back up as the idea behind the cryptocurrency was just getting started. You should do the same.

Fastest Growing

Bitcoins were the fastest growing investment introduced in the new millennium. This is because they went from being worth $0 to being worth over $1,000 in just seven years. The Bitcoin industry went from nothing to booming during that time and people were able to make a lot of the money back that they initially put into Bitcoins.

It has been declared as the fastest growing investment and predictions put it at having unlimited growth potential. Eventually, a single Bitcoin could be worth into the millions.

Competitors

There have been so many competitors of the Bitcoin that they had to start coming up with a name to group them all together. While Bitcoin was the first to *coin* the term cryptocurrency, it is now used for Bitcoin and the competitors that it has.

While there are competitors on the market that are trying to become as big as Bitcoin, not a single one of them has been able to see even a fraction of the growth that Bitcoin has seen.

Other forms of cryptocurrency include things like "Lite Coins" and Ethereum. None of them have really been able to compete with Bitcoin because of the market that Bitcoin now dominates and because of the way that the system is set up to ensure that Bitcoin is going to be the biggest and best option on the market.

There can be cryptocurrency and they can try to compete with Bitcoin but, unless there is a huge shift in the market, there won't ever be another Bitcoin.

No Replication

Unlike real money, there is no way to replicate Bitcoin. This involves the coding process that comes around when Bitcoin are created. Since they all have a unique code that is attached to them, it would be impossible for anyone to make a copy of a Bitcoin.

This is one thing that is especially promising for banks and other financial professionals. With Bitcoin, there is no way to make counterfeit. Despite all of the technology (or, perhaps, because of all of it), there is still a huge problem with counterfeit money throughout the world. Bitcoin eliminates all of that.

Bitcoin Cash

In 2016, Vancouver in Canada became the first state to officially have an ATM where you could get cash for your Bitcoin. Just like the selling model that is online, you will need to pay a fee to be able to get that cash but it adds an extra level of convenience for people who have Bitcoin and who want to be able to get the cold, hard cash for the Bitcoin that they have worked so hard to collect.

Expect to pay slightly more than the normal selling fee that you would find on a site if you want to be able to cash out your Bitcoin using an ATM-style machine.

Buying Cars

If you want to buy a car from an individual seller, you might be able to pay in Bitcoin. The availability of Bitcoin for cars and things similar really depends on the person who is selling it and if they are selling it in an individualized format. There were no big dealerships or car brands that offered buyers the chance to buy cars in Bitcoin until one company stepped up and decided that they could make some extra money by allowing people to buy their cars with Bitcoin.

This company was none other than luxury genius car company, Lamborghini. They now accept Bitcoin at every one of their dealerships across the United States and in other countries.

You can also pay on their website with your Bitcoin if you are creating a completely customized version of your dream car. When you pay with Bitcoin at Lamborghini, you can also expect to be able to pay for all of your services that they perform. Oil changes, car washes, and services can all be paid for with Bitcoin at Lamborghini dealerships.

Ban on Bitcoin

There is no place in the world that has an official ban on Bitcoin in the traditional sense. You will not go to jail for getting caught with Bitcoin but banks in China could face serious problems if they allow the trade of Bitcoin to happen at the bank.

It is important to note that China created a ban on Bitcoin training for banks. Individuals are still allowed to trade Bitcoin for the time being and they will continue to be allowed to do so if there are no problems with Bitcoin.

Banks in China face charges, fines, and possible closures if they allow Bitcoin trading within the bank. The reasoning for this is China feels that Bitcoin is more of a currency than a trading item. They want to make sure that people are not trading "money" through the bank and that everyone is being treated fairly when it comes to their opportunity to trade Bitcoin.

China simply does not want banks to take up all of the positive parts of Bitcoin and take them away from people who have sold them.

New Bitcoin

Whether you are interested in mining or not, it may be the way to go if you are looking for a fortune in Bitcoin. Each day that there is Bitcoin mining going on, there are 3,600 new Bitcoins created. That is the equivalent of nearly $400,000 — just shy of half of a million. While you should know that you won't be able to find *all* the Bitcoins in one day while you are mining, it is something that is worth looking into for the Bitcoin fortune that you want to amass.

Now, what will it be? Are you buying your Bitcoin, mining it or trading it for something that you have to sell? The options for Bitcoin investment are limitless as is the potential for growth of the investment return!

Conclusion

Thank for making it through to the end of *Bitcoin: what you need to know about the cryptocurrency.* Let's hope it was informative and able to provide you with all of the tools you need to achieve your goals of making money with Bitcoin and learning how to profit from the different types of Bitcoin investing.

The next step is to find one of the many Bitcoin sites and explore what they have to offer you. You will be able to learn the different aspects of investing and that will help you to get where you need to go with your Bitcoin investment. You can also learn the different prices of Bitcoin and how they fluctuate on a regular basis.

Then, you will be ready to buy your first Bitcoin and begin making money.

Finally, if you found this book useful in any way, a review on Amazon is always appreciated!

Do you have any feedback or typo to report?

Email me at bresettmark@gmail.com.

Made in the USA
Lexington, KY
16 August 2017